The Usborne Nature Trail Book of
PONDS & STREAMS

Written by Su Swallow and Margaret Stephens
Edited by Ingrid Selberg
Consultant Editor Alfred Leutscher BSc, FZS
Special Advice from Peter Holden, Chris Humphries,
Alwyne Wheeler, Anthony Wootten.
Editorial revision by Margaret Stephens
Designed by Sally Burrough
Design revision by Diane Thistlethwaite and Robert Walster

Illustrated by
John Barber, Amanda Barlow, Joyce Bee, Isabel Bowring,
Hilary Burn, Don Forrest, Christine Howes, Ian Jackson,
Annabel Milne, Richard Orr, Gillian Platt, Annabel Spenceley,
Peter Stebbing, Phil Weare and John Yates.

The fresh water of ponds and streams is a home or hunting ground for many living creatures and plants.

There you will spot the common birds, fish, insects, mammals, plants and amphibians of Europe, all described in this part of the book.

As you turn these pages, you will discover how water animals and plants live and how to collect wild specimens and keep them at home for study.

To identify your fresh-water wildlife, turn to the pages which deal with the kind of animal or plant you have seen. If you can't find a picture of it there, turn to the section called *More freshwater life you can spot* and you may find a picture of it there.

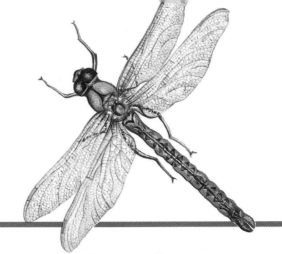

The Usborne Nature Trail Book of
PONDS & STREAMS

Contents

First published in 1977 by
Usborne Publishing Ltd,
Usborne House,
83-85 Saffron Hill,
London EC1N 8RT
United Kingdom

Printed in Belgium

How to start

The best time to study streams and ponds is in the spring and summer, when the plants are flowering and the animals are most active. Winter can be a good time to spot birds though.

Always move slowly and quietly and be careful your shadow does not disturb fish. You will find more wildlife near the bank, where there is more plant cover.

Freshwater life can be found in lakes, rivers, ditches and canals, as well. You may even find plants and insects in rainwater tubs.

Be responsible!

Plants and animals live in harmony with each other and their surroundings. If you remove many plants and animals then you will upset the balance and threaten the survival of some of those that are left behind (see page 167). If you destroy their surroundings (their habitat), you will threaten their survival as well. Never leave litter behind when you leave.

What to take

Clean jam jars

Empty margarine pot for putting animals in and watching them.

Magnifying glass

Fishing net with small mesh.

Binoculars

Safety first

Never go into the water if you cannot swim and only go into shallow water. Do not wade rivers or deep streams. There may be strong currents. Always take a friend or adult with you. If you do fall in and get wet, go straight home to change you clothes and get dry - unless of course it is a very hot sunny day.

A pond survey

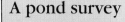

With some friends, make a map of your pond, showing where you found certain plants and animals. Note down the types of things going on around the pond and what it is used for, such as boating and fishing, or if cattle drink there. How do all these activities affect the pond? Check for signs of pollution, such as litter and oil.

Note down the animals you see. Record every kind of plant you can see. Look for insects on the plants.

What to look for

Even a small pond or stream can have many plants and animals, if it is not too shaded or polluted. Here are some of the plants you should look for and their hiding places.

Damselfly

Look under water plants for eggs and small animals.

Great Diving Beetle

In a stream, look under stones for worms, insects and leeches. In a pond, the gaps beneath stones tend to get silted up, so you will not find much wildlife beneath them.

Mayfly nymph

Do's and don'ts

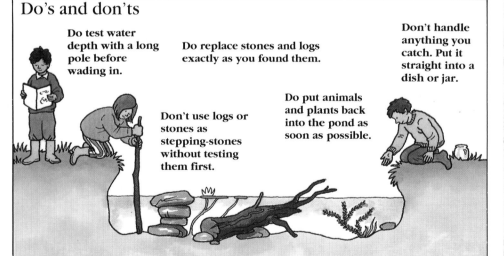

Do test water depth with a long pole before wading in.

Do replace stones and logs exactly as you found them.

Don't handle anything you catch. Put it straight into a dish or jar.

Don't use logs or stones as stepping-stones without testing them first.

Do put animals and plants back into the pond as soon as possible.

Don't stamp your feet or move quickly. This will frighten animals.

Don't take too many animals or whole plants. Part of a plant will be enough to identify it.

Don't smash ice on ponds in winter. This will disturb animals living there.

Do keep jars with specimens in the shade, to keep the water cool.

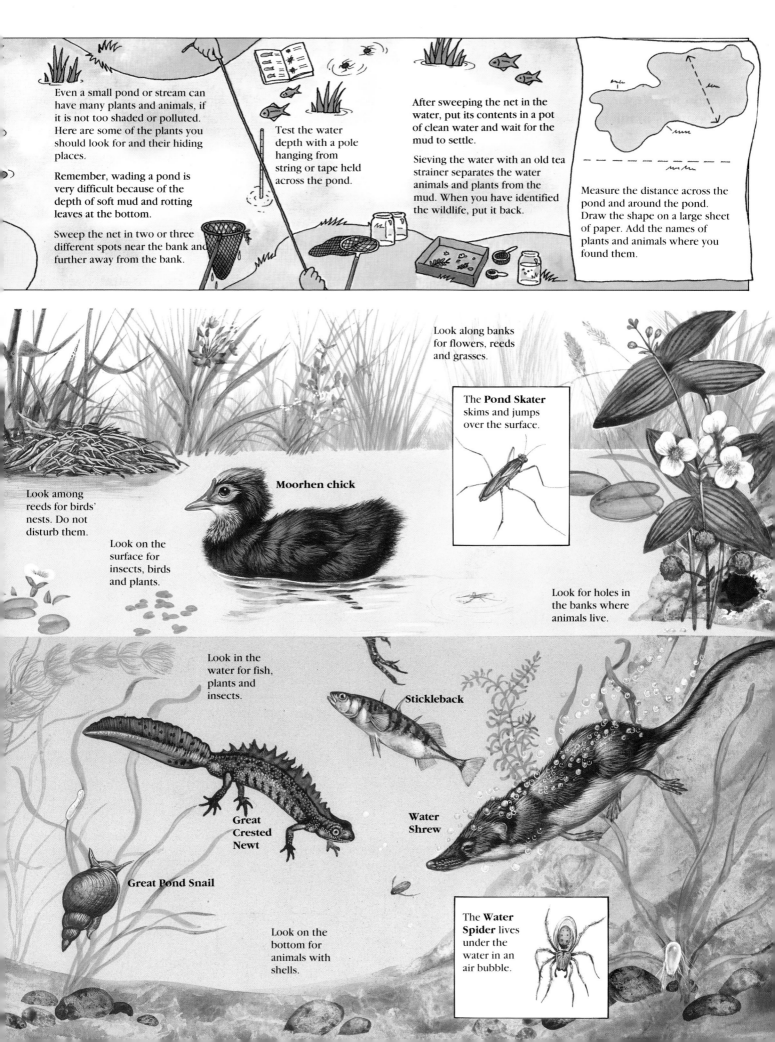

Even a small pond or stream can have many plants and animals, if it is not too shaded or polluted. Here are some of the plants you should look for and their hiding places.

Remember, wading a pond is very difficult because of the depth of soft mud and rotting leaves at the bottom.

Sweep the net in two or three different spots near the bank and further away from the bank.

Test the water depth with a pole hanging from string or tape held across the pond.

After sweeping the net in the water, put its contents in a pot of clean water and wait for the mud to settle.

Sieving the water with an old tea strainer separates the water animals and plants from the mud. When you have identified the wildlife, put it back.

Measure the distance across the pond and around the pond. Draw the shape on a large sheet of paper. Add the names of plants and animals where you found them.

Look along banks for flowers, reeds and grasses.

The Pond Skater skims and jumps over the surface.

Look among reeds for birds' nests. Do not disturb them.

Look on the surface for insects, birds and plants.

Moorhen chick

Look for holes in the banks where animals live.

Look in the water for fish, plants and insects.

Stickleback

Water Shrew

Great Crested Newt

Great Pond Snail

Look on the bottom for animals with shells.

The **Water Spider** lives under the water in an air bubble.

Living together

In a thriving pond there is a balance of different kinds of animals and plants, so that there is enough food for them all to survive. It is important not to disturb this balance.

How plants help

Animals need a gas called oxygen to survive. Water animals can get oxygen from the surface and some from the water itself. Oxygen in the water comes from the water plants.

Plants need sunlight to make food and produce their oxygen.

Canadian Pondweed

Try this experiment. Put some Canadian Pondweed in water and leave it in the sun. Oxygen bubbles will soon appear.

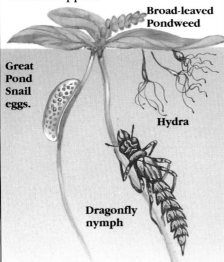

Broad-leaved Pondweed

Great Pond Snail eggs.

Hydra

Dragonfly nymph

Plants can provide animals with shade and shelter from enemies. They act as a support for eggs, such as those of the Great Pond Snail. Some tiny animals cling on to plants, such as the Hydra, which catch prey swimming by. Insects, such as the Dragonfly, use plant stems to climb out of the water when they are ready to become adults.

Pond food chains

The process of big animals eating smaller animals, which in turn eat even smaller animals, is called a food chain. In the food chain here, the Heron is at the top and eats animals in the second link, such as Perch. Perch eat animals in the third link and so the chain progresses down to algae in the fifth link.

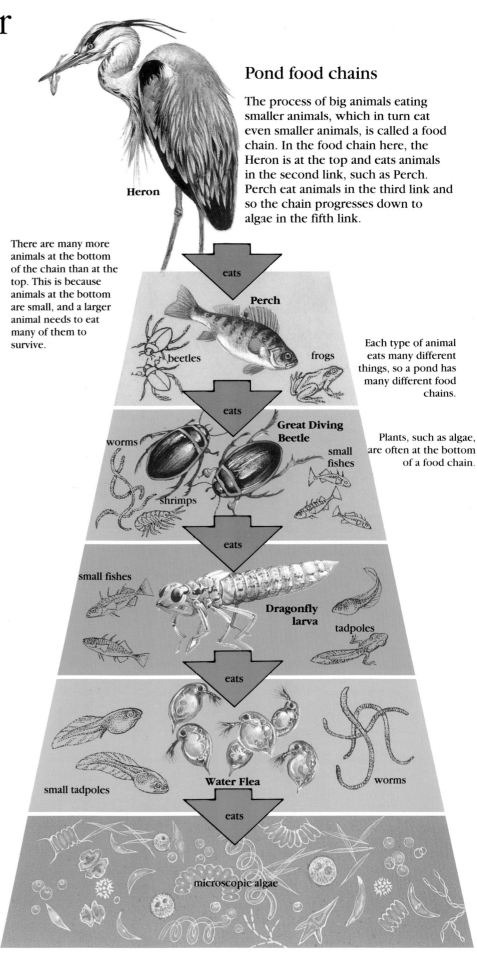

Heron

There are many more animals at the bottom of the chain than at the top. This is because animals at the bottom are small, and a larger animal needs to eat many of them to survive.

eats

Perch

beetles   frogs

eats

worms   **Great Diving Beetle**

shrimps   small fishes

eats

small fishes   **Dragonfly larva**   tadpoles

eats

small tadpoles   **Water Flea**   worms

eats

microscopic algae

Each type of animal eats many different things, so a pond has many different food chains.

Plants, such as algae, are often at the bottom of a food chain.

Pollution

Human beings have a lot to answer for. Their pollution is a serious threat to the plants and animals living in the fresh water of rivers, ponds and streams. Here are some of the ways, not all man made though, that fresh water can become polluted. Phosphates from detergents in the home, such as those used to wash clothes, pass through sewage works and into fresh water. Phosphates cause water plants to grow strongly. When they die, the plants are broken up by bacteria which use up all the oxygen in the water. Water animals need oxygen to live, so this lack of oxygen can kill them. Human sewage entering rivers is also broken up by bacteria which starve the rivers of oxygen. Another problem from sewage is that it can cause fungus to grow which kills off plants.

The stream is usually clear and unpolluted at its source.

Mining waste floats on the surface, blocking out the light which plants need to make food. Some pieces of waste settle into spaces in the river bed where animals live.

Burning fossil fuels, such as petrol in cars and coal in power stations, releases sulphur and nitrogen into the air. These two gases make the rain more acid. This acid rain falls into fresh water and can kill fish.

Farmers use fertilizers on their land to grow more crops Some of these chemicals are washed off the land by rain into fresh water, or seep through the ground into fresh water. Fertilizers can make water plants grow faster and bigger. The more decaying plants there are, the less oxygen there is for water animals to breath. Algae grows faster and bigger too. This can cause the water to become murky and so cut off light from water plants growing at the bottom.

Poisons and chemical from factories are released into rivers. These can kill fish and make the water smell bad.

Water sports, such as boating and water skiing can disturb animal and plant life and damage river banks.

Overhanging tress block out the light from water plants and stop them growing. Fallen leaves from the trees use up much oxygen as they rot by the activity of bacteria. This is not a man made problem, but it can be solved by humans cutting back the trees.

Rain running off large heaps of manure can poison fish.

Rubbish dumped into ponds poisons the water and kills pond life. Water birds can get trapped by rubbish, such as string and wire, and die.

Plants of ponds and streams

Different types of plants grow in different areas or zones in a pond and around its edges. Remember that zones can often overlap and that you may not find all the zones shown here in one pond. Many of these freshwater plants also grow in streams and rivers.

Notice how delicate many of the plants in deep water are. They do not need thick stems to support them, because they are held up by the water. Their leaves are fine and thin because they do not need to hold water as land plants do.

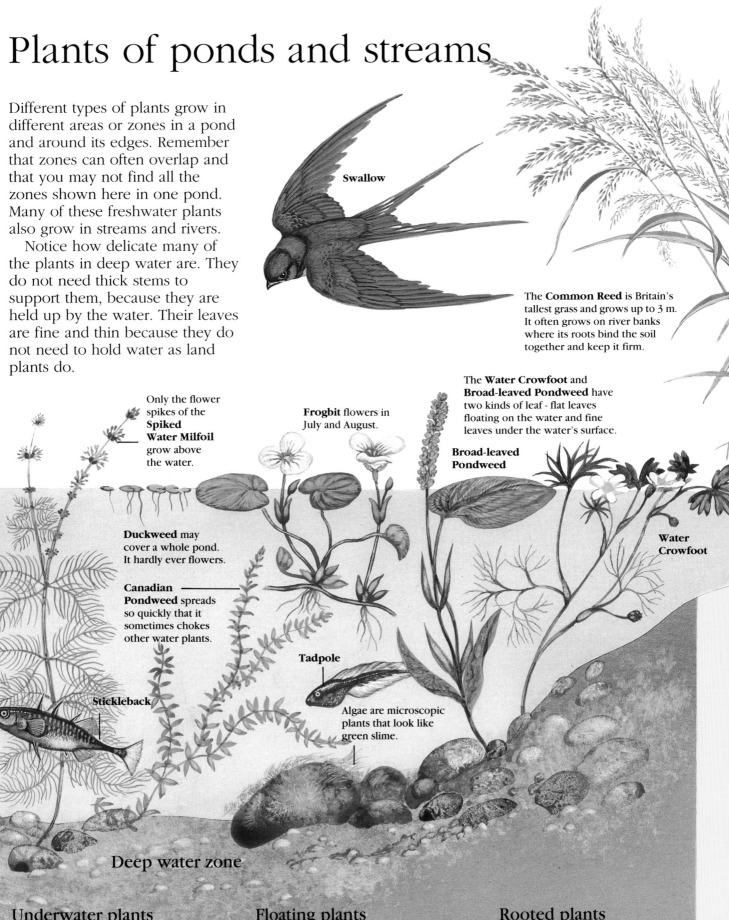

Swallow

The **Common Reed** is Britain's tallest grass and grows up to 3 m. It often grows on river banks where its roots bind the soil together and keep it firm.

The **Water Crowfoot** and **Broad-leaved Pondweed** have two kinds of leaf - flat leaves floating on the water and fine leaves under the water's surface.

Only the flower spikes of the **Spiked Water Milfoil** grow above the water.

Frogbit flowers in July and August.

Broad-leaved Pondweed

Duckweed may cover a whole pond. It hardly ever flowers.

Canadian Pondweed spreads so quickly that it sometimes chokes other water plants.

Water Crowfoot

Tadpole

Algae are microscopic plants that look like green slime.

Stickleback

Deep water zone

Underwater plants

In the middle of the pond, plants grow under water, except some of the flower heads which can rise above the surface. Plant roots here are anchored in the mud.

Floating plants

Some plants that grow near the centre of the pond, such as the Frogbit, have roots that are not anchored at the bottom. They float freely in the water.

Rooted plants

Plants that grow in fairly shallow water around the edges of this zone have their roots in the mud. Their leaves can float or they stand out of the water.

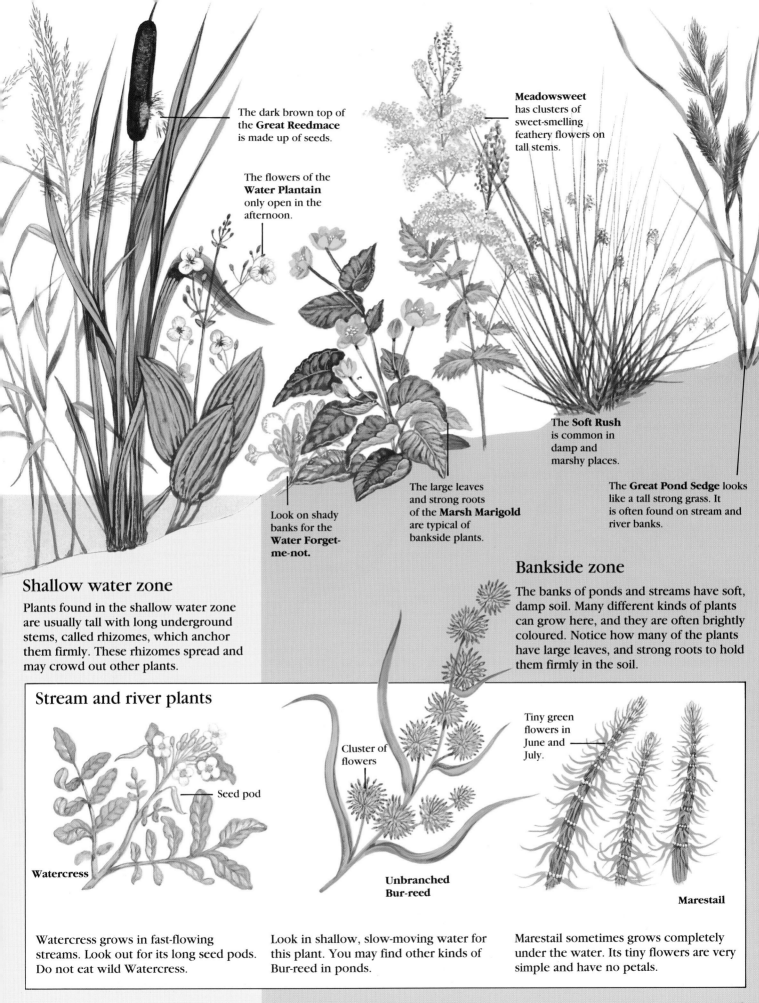

The dark brown top of the **Great Reedmace** is made up of seeds.

The flowers of the **Water Plantain** only open in the afternoon.

Meadowsweet has clusters of sweet-smelling feathery flowers on tall stems.

Look on shady banks for the **Water Forget-me-not.**

The large leaves and strong roots of the **Marsh Marigold** are typical of bankside plants.

The **Soft Rush** is common in damp and marshy places.

The **Great Pond Sedge** looks like a tall strong grass. It is often found on stream and river banks.

Shallow water zone

Plants found in the shallow water zone are usually tall with long underground stems, called rhizomes, which anchor them firmly. These rhizomes spread and may crowd out other plants.

Bankside zone

The banks of ponds and streams have soft, damp soil. Many different kinds of plants can grow here, and they are often brightly coloured. Notice how many of the plants have large leaves, and strong roots to hold them firmly in the soil.

Stream and river plants

Seed pod

Watercress

Cluster of flowers

Unbranched Bur-reed

Tiny green flowers in June and July.

Marestail

Watercress grows in fast-flowing streams. Look out for its long seed pods. Do not eat wild Watercress.

Look in shallow, slow-moving water for this plant. You may find other kinds of Bur-reed in ponds.

Marestail sometimes grows completely under the water. Its tiny flowers are very simple and have no petals.

9

How water plants grow

Many water plants grow from seeds. The seeds are formed after pollen from the male part of the flower (the stamen) reaches the female part (the ovary) of the same kind of plant. When the seeds are ripe, they scatter from the parent plant and can grow into new plants. Some water plants can also spread by sending out underground stems (rhizomes).

Some underwater plants do not spread by seed at all. Instead, new plants grow from winter buds or from pieces that break off the parent plant.

How pollen is scattered

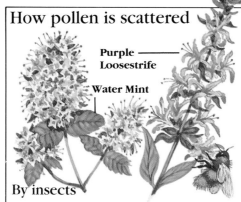

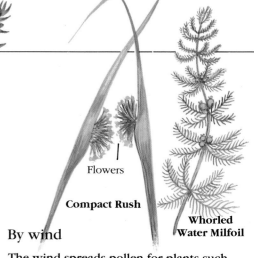

By insects

In some plants, pollen is spread by insects. The flowers' bright colours and scent attract the insects. The pollen rubs off on to their bodies and they carry it to other plants.

By wind

The wind spreads pollen for plants such as these. Their flowers are often small and dull. This is because they do not need to attract insects to spread the pollen.

How seeds are scattered

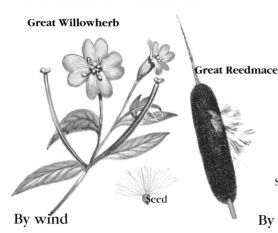

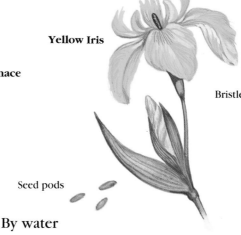

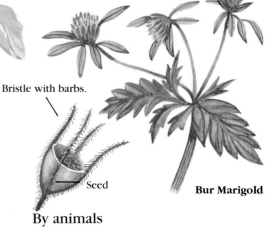

By wind

Some seeds are carried by the wind on a hairy parachute. Great Willowherb seeds may travel as faraway as 150 km.

By water

Some seeds, like the ones in these Yellow Iris pods, are carried by water. The pods open when softened by water.

By animals

Seeds with barbs, or hooks, catch on to the fur of animals or people's clothing, as they brush past. Later they drop off.

How Water Lilies grow

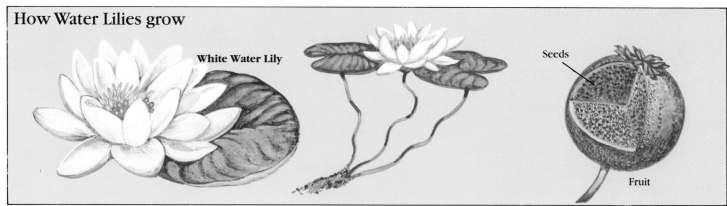

Look in ponds for the White Water Lily. Its leaves and flowers float on the water's surface. At night, the flowers close and sometimes sink just below the surface until morning.

The plant is anchored to the bottom by stout rhizomes. The stalks grow at an angle. If the water level rises, the stalks can straighten up so that the flowers and leaves still float.

The flowers spread their pollen by insects. When the fruits are ripe, they sink to the bottom and release up to 2,000 seeds. The seeds float away. Some sink and grow into new plants.

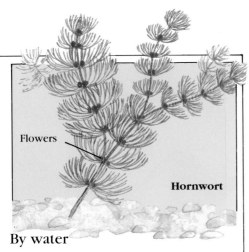

Flowers

Hornwort

By water

This plant flowers and spreads its pollen under the water. The male flowers release pollen into the water. Some of it settles on the female flowers and pollinates them.

Another way that water plants spread.

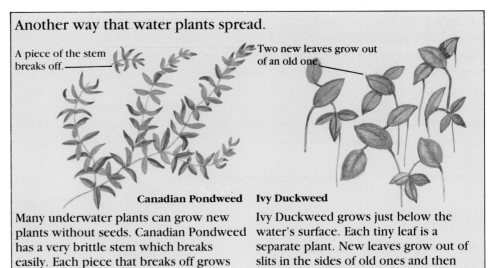

A piece of the stem breaks off.

Two new leaves grow out of an old one.

Canadian Pondweed

Ivy Duckweed

Many underwater plants can grow new plants without seeds. Canadian Pondweed has a very brittle stem which breaks easily. Each piece that breaks off grows into a new plant.

Ivy Duckweed grows just below the water's surface. Each tiny leaf is a separate plant. New leaves grow out of slits in the sides of old ones and then break away to become new plants.

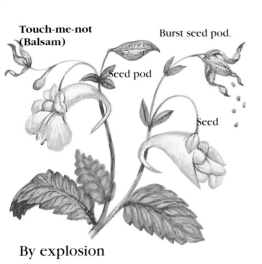

Touch-me-not (Balsam)

Burst seed pod.

Seed pod

Seed

By explosion

If anything touches the ripe seed pods of this plant, they burst open and scatter the seeds on the ground.

Watching a plant grow

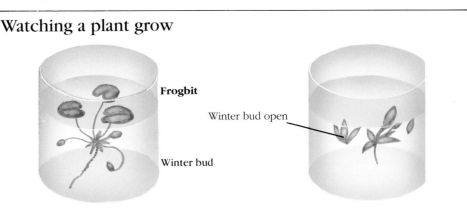

Frogbit

Winter bud

Winter bud open

Frogbit grows winter buds on underwater roots. Each bud contains a new plant and a store of food. When the buds are ripe, they break off and sink. In spring, when the stored food is used up, the buds float to the surface and grow into new plants. Collect some Frogbit in the autumn and watch how it grows. Place it in a jar of pond water and keep it cool.

In winter

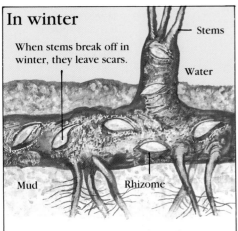

Stems

When stems break off in winter, they leave scars.

Water

Mud

Rhizome

In winter, plants such as the White Water Lily die down. They live off food stored in their rhizomes. In spring, new stems grow up from the rhizomes.

Insect-eating plants

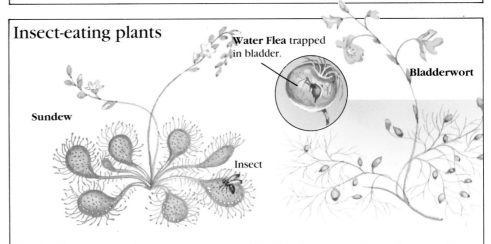

Water Flea trapped in bladder.

Bladderwort

Sundew

Insect

The Sundew grows in bogs and marshes where the soil is very poor. It gets food by trapping insects on its hairy leaves and digests them with special juices.

The Bladderwort is also an insect-eating plant. It catches its tiny prey in underwater bladders which are filled with air. Then it feeds on them.

Watching water birds

Birdwatching by ponds and streams is exciting because you can see so many different types. Some birds spend most of their lives on or by water. Others may come just to drink and bathe. In winter, you may spot sea birds as they shelter and search for food inland.

The best place to look for birds is by water surrounded by thick vegetation. Early in the morning is a good time to see them. In parks, some water birds are tame enough to be fed. Others are shy, so you must hide and wait quietly to see them. Keep a record of the birds you spot and their habits. If you find a nest, be sure not to disturb it.

Feeding

Watch the birds on or around a pond closely. Spot the different ways they feed and the shapes of their bills. Each bill is shaped to suit a different way of feeding. Time how long a diving duck can stay under the water.

Mallards are dabbling ducks. They feed near the surface and eat mostly plants. They also up-end to get food from deep water.

Tufted Ducks dive down 1 m or 2 m for water plants, insects and small fish.

Female   Male

Wigeon feed mainly on grasses and grain, cropped from fields. They also dabble in water.

The **Swift** feeds and even sleeps on the wing. It eats flies and beetles.

The **Shoveler** uses its wide bill to sieve food from water and mud.

The **Bittern** nests in reed beds where it is camouflaged well. It eats frogs, small fish and insects.

The **Teal** is Britain's smallest duck. It is a surface-feeder and eats mainly water plants and their seeds.

The **Moorhen** eats plants and small animals in the water as well as seeds and grain on land.

The **Kingfisher** dives for small fish and insects. It sometimes beats a fish against a branch to kill it. Then it swallows the fish head first, so that the fins and scales do not open and choke the bird.

Flocks in flight

Geese in V-shape.

Ducks in straight line.

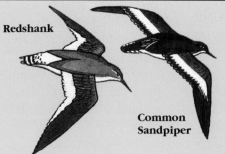

Redshank

Common Sandpiper

Taking a count

Count the first ten birds in a flock. Then estimate how many sets of ten there might be altogether. Multiply your estimated figure by 10 to get the total number of birds.

Flight patterns

Different sorts of birds fly in different flock patterns. These patterns can help you to identify the birds. Many birds fly in a line or a'V-shape. See if you can spot other patterns.

Keeping together

Birds that fly in flocks usually have special markings for others to follow. They also call to each other so that they keep the flock together, especially after dark.

The **Greylag Goose** spends a lot of time on land. It crops the grass with its bill.

Looking after feathers

Goosander

Great Crested Grebe

Bathing

Water birds often bathe to keep clean. They flap their wings on the water and roll over to wet their bodies thoroughly. Then they shake themselves dry.

Oiling

Next, the birds rub oil over the feathers with their bills and heads. The oil comes from the preen glands near their tails. It keeps the feathers in good condition and waterproofs them.

Pintail

Preening

Finally, they fluff up their feathers, nibble each one and draw them through their bills. This cleans and oils the feathers even more, and settles them back into place.

How feathers work

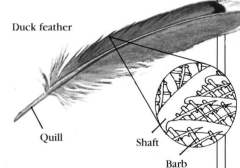

Duck feather

Quill

Shaft

Barb

The barbs on a bird's feather grow out of the shaft. They fit together very closely, rather like the teeth of a zip. This helps keep the bird's body dry and warm.

Birds - mating and nesting

Birds become very active in the spring when most of them breed. The male birds attract the females by showing off their bright feathers. Some develop crests and ruffs of feathers at this time. They also have special mating calls and can perform acrobatics in the air or on the water. Sometimes both male and female birds take part in these courtship displays.

After the female accepts the male as her mate, a nest is built. See if you can spot which materials each kind of bird collects for its nest.

Courtship

Great Crested Grebes start their courtship early in the year. Head-shaking (above) is a common display. The birds swim towards each other, calling and shaking their heads from side to side.

After head-shaking, the Grebes may "dance" together. First they dive to collect weed. Then they swim towards one another and rise out of the water, swaying their bills and paddling hard.

Fighting

Mute Swan

Greylag Goose

Coots

This Mute Swan is puffing out its feathers. This makes the bird look bigger and helps to frighten away enemies. Some birds fight to defend their nest or territory.

This Greylag Goose is standing in a threat position and probably hissing to chase away other adult geese that dare to come too close to its nest or territory.

Coots fight with their claws, holding themselves up with their wings. Fights do not last very long, and usually only the males take part.

Nesting

Reed Warblers

Sand Martins

Dipper

The Reed Warbler nests in reed beds. The grass nest is shaped like a deep basket, so that the eggs and young birds do not fall out, even in a strong wind.

Look for groups of Sand Martins nesting in mud or sand banks. Each nest is at the end of a tunnel, which the birds dig with their feet and bills.

The Dipper hides its nest in cracks in rocks near a stream, under a bridge or behind a waterfall. The cup-shaped nest is made of moss and grasses.

Female
Male

Kingfishers

Male

Female

Pochards

Male

Mallards

Female

During courtship, some male birds, such as the Kingfisher, offer the females a present of food. When the female has accepted her present, this means she is ready to mate.

The Mallard is a common duck, so you have a very good chance of seeing the male's striking courtship display. He dives, flaps his wings, sprays water from his bill, whistles and grunts. The female

attracts the male by jerking her head backwards and forwards. The male Pochard swims around the female and jerks his head backwards and forwards to attract her.

Looking after the young

Grey Herons

Some birds, such as the Grey Heron, are born helpless. They are blind, have no feathers, and cannot leave the nest for over a month. The young beg for food by pecking at their parents' bills.

Other types of young bird beg for food with loud cries or gaping beaks. Some birds, such as ducks and grebes, have feathers and can swim and feed a few hours after hatching.

Keeping the young safe

Little Grebes (or **Dabchicks**)

Little Grebe chicks can swim soon after they hatch. Sometimes they climb on to their parents' backs to keep safe from danger.

Little Ringed Plover

Like many birds that nest on the ground, the Little Ringed Plover moves away from the nest pretending to be hurt to divert an enemy from its young and eggs.

Watching water insects

When you visit a pond or stream, you will soon spot several different types of insects. Look in the air, on the water's surface and in the water itself. To help you to identify an insect, note down its colour, the shape and number of its wings, where you saw it, and any other details.

All adult insects have bodies with three parts, three pairs of legs, and usually a pair of antennae or feelers. Many have wings at some time in their lives.

Most insects breathe by taking in air through holes in their bodies. Many underwater insects carry a bubble of air on their bodies, which they collect at the surface.

Above the water

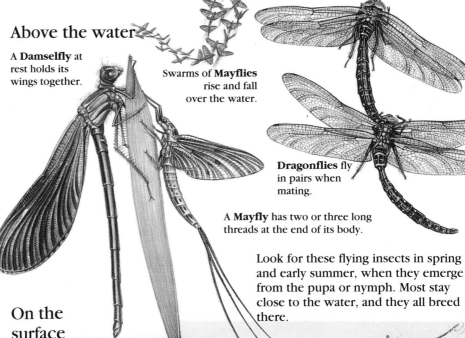

A **Damselfly** at rest holds its wings together.

Swarms of **Mayflies** rise and fall over the water.

Dragonflies fly in pairs when mating.

A **Mayfly** has two or three long threads at the end of its body.

Look for these flying insects in spring and early summer, when they emerge from the pupa or nymph. Most stay close to the water, and they all breed there.

On the surface

A thin film on the water's surface stops an insect from sinking. See how this works by floating a needle on water.

Place some blotting paper on the surface of some water. Now place a needle on the blotting paper.

Watch the needle stay on the surface as the blotting paper soaks up water and sinks.

The **Water Boatman** swims and takes in air at the surface, upside down. It has a sharp bite when picked up.

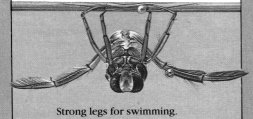

Strong legs for swimming.

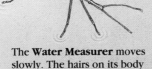

The **Water Measurer** moves slowly. The hairs on its body stop it from getting wet.

Tiny **Springtails** can jump 30 cm, using their hinged tails.

The **Pond Skater** slides rapidly over the surface. It can also jump.

Whirligig Beetles have one pair of eyes looking into the water, and another pair looking into the air. They whirl and spin while hunting for food.

Notice the different ways that these insects move on the water's surface. They feed mostly on dead insects that fall on the water.

Under the water

Breathing tube

The antenna breaks the surface film of the water while it collects air.

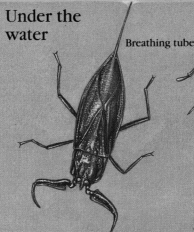

Air bubble

The **Water Scorpion** is not a real scorpion at all. It takes in air at the surface through a breathing tube. It stores air under its wing cases.

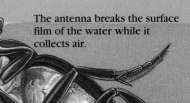

The **Great Silver Beetle** carries a bubble of air trapped by the hairs on its underside.

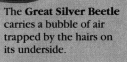

16

How insects feed

Young **Stickleback**

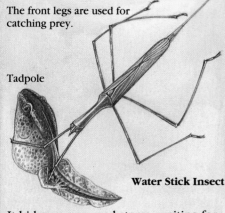

Great Diving Beetle

Many water beetles eat other animals. The Great Diving Beetle feeds on tadpoles, insects and small fish. Its prey can sometimes be larger than itself.

The front legs are used for catching prey.

Tadpole

Water Stick Insect

It hides among reed stems, waiting for prey. The front legs shoot out to catch animals, such as insects and tadpoles. Then it sucks out their juices.

The Lesser Water Boatman feeds on algae and rotting plants on the bottom. Unlike the Water Boatman, it swims with its right side up.

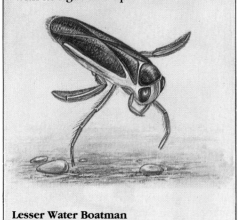

Lesser Water Boatman

Making an insect aquarium

This picture shows the things you will need to make an aquarium. Keep the aquarium near a window, but not in direct sunlight. If you use tap water, add some pond water and leave it for a few days before adding the animals. Do not fill it too deep and add snails to keep the sides from being covered in algae.

Nymphs and larvae

Feed nymphs and larvae on worms or tiny bits of raw meat. Remove uneaten pieces of meat or the water will become unpleasant.

Clean waterproof tank. (A plastic or glass bowl will do.)

Pond or tap water.

Twig for nymphs to climb on to.

Stones

Snail

Washed sand or gravel 5 cm deep.

Flying insects

To keep flying insects, such as beetles, put a lid or some fine netting over the aquarium to stop them from escaping.

Glass or plastic cover resting on small pieces of wood.

Leave a gap for air to get in.

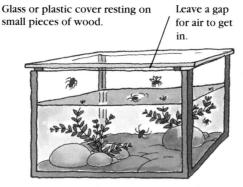

Feed beetles on worms or tiny bits of raw meat.

Tiny insects

Keep these insects in separate containers, or they will eat each other. Feed them on pieces of meat or worms.

Lid with air holes.

Margarine pot

Clear plastic cover with air holes.

Rubber band

Magnifying glass

Fierce insects

Keep tiny insects in a jar or pot. Put in pond water, some mud and a few plants. Do not forget to make air holes in the clear plastic cover or the jar's lid.

Great Diving Beetle

Water Stick Insect

Water Scorpion

Water Boatman

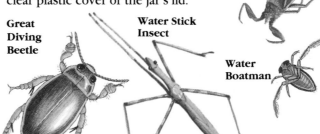

Remember!

Only take a few insects from the water. Make sure they have the right food and enough room. Always return them to the pond or stream when you have finished studying them.

How insects grow

You can find some exciting insects in ponds and streams, even in polluted water. Most insects go through several stages of development from the egg to adult. (Follow the life cycle of the Caddis Fly in this section.) The early stages may last for years, but the adult may only live for a few hours or days.

Some water insects, such as water beetles, spend all their lives in the water. Others, such as the Alder Fly, leave the water when fully grown.

The Caddis Fly

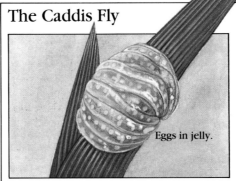

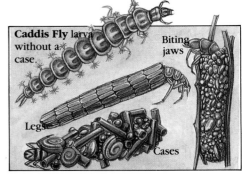

Eggs in jelly.

Caddis Fly larva without a case.

Biting jaws

Legs

Cases

Egg

The Caddis Fly begins its life in fresh water. The eggs are laid in jelly on plants or stones, either above or below the water's surface.

Larva

The larva hatches from the egg. Then it may make a protective case of shells, stones or leaves. The larva eats plants from the bottom of the pond.

Where insects lay eggs

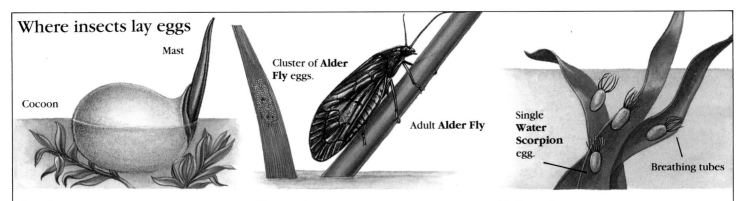

Mast

Cocoon

Cluster of **Alder Fly** eggs.

Adult **Alder Fly**

Single **Water Scorpion** egg.

Breathing tubes

On the water

The Great Silver Beetle lays its eggs in a silky cocoon on the surface of the water. The hollow "mast" of the cocoon allows air to reach the eggs.

Above the water

Look for insect eggs on water plants and stones above the water's surface. When the larvae hatch, they fall or crawl down into the water.

Below the water

Some insects lay their eggs under the water on plants or stones, or on the mud bottom. The Water Scorpion lays its eggs on plant stems.

Larvae and nymphs

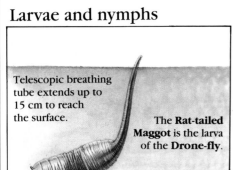

Telescopic breathing tube extends up to 15 cm to reach the surface.

The **Rat-tailed Maggot** is the larva of the **Drone-fly**.

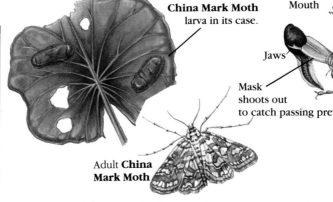

China Mark Moth larva in its case.

Adult **China Mark Moth**

Mouth

Jaws

Mask shoots out to catch passing prey.

Dragonfly nymph

Put some mud from a pond or stream into a dish. Add a little water and sieve it with an old tea strainer. See if you can spot the Rat-tailed Maggot and its breathing tube.

Look for small holes in the leaves of Water Lilies and Pondweed. Underneath the leaves, you may see this moth larva, which makes a case out of the leaves and also feeds on them.

A young dragonfly is called a nymph when it hatches from the egg. It has a strong pair of jaws fixed to a hinge, called a mask. See how the adult emerges from the nymph on page 19.

Caddis Fly pupa develops inside a case.

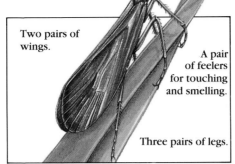

Two pairs of wings.

A pair of feelers for touching and smelling.

Three pairs of legs.

Pupa

After about a year, the larva stops eating and changes into a pupa. Over a period of time, the pupa then slowly changes into an adult Caddis Fly.

Adult

When the adult is fully grown, the pupa leaves its case, if it has one, and moves to the surface. Then the adult splits out of its pupal skin and flies away.

An underwater viewer

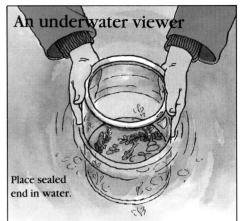

Place sealed end in water.

Use a large clean plastic sweet jar that you can see through. Remove the lid. Place the bottom of the jar in the water and look through the top.

A Dragonfly emerges

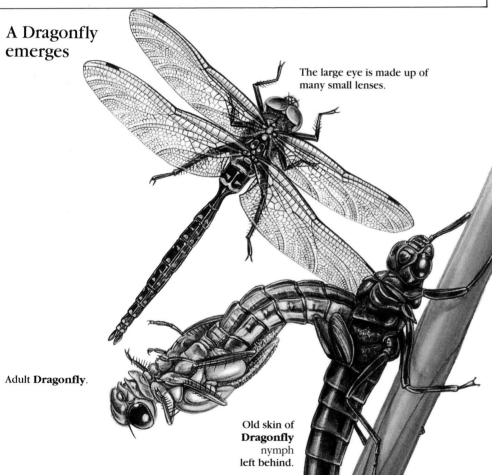

The large eye is made up of many small lenses.

Adult **Dragonfly**.

Old skin of **Dragonfly** nymph left behind.

Water surface

Adult Dragonflies emerge in summer. First, the brown nymph crawls out of the water and onto a plant stem. Then its skin splits down the back and the adult Dragonfly slowly pulls itself out, head first. It rests on the plant while its body hardens and the wings expand. Then it flies away. Dragonflies only live for about a month.

Watching Gnats grow

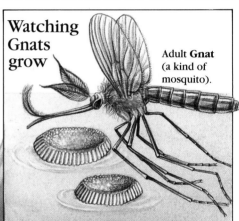

Adult **Gnat** (a kind of mosquito).

Egg rafts (about 5 mm long).

In early summer, look on the surface of still water for Gnat eggs, which look like tiny rafts. Keep some out of doors in a jar of pond water.

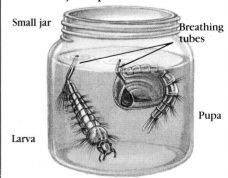

Small jar

Breathing tubes

Pupa

Larva

The larva changes into a pupa after about three weeks. The pupa develops into an adult. Then the pupal skin splits open and the adult flies away.

Mammals

Most mammals that live near fresh water are very shy and you will not see them often. All you hear is a plop as they jump into the water. Some only come out at night. They are called nocturnal mammals.

Mammals can hear well and have a good sense of smell. So if you go animal tracking, approach the water quietly, facing the wind. If you find animal tracks or feeding signs, try to identify them. Then you will know which animal you are following.

Spot the difference

Water Vole

Tiny ears

Blunt snout

Short, furry tail.

Brown Rat

Large ears

Pointed snout

Long, naked tail.

The Water Vole is often confused with the Brown Rat. They look rather alike and both are often seen swimming. Look at the differences carefully, so that you can tell them apart if you spot them. The Water Vole often swims under the water, but the Brown Rat keeps more to the surface of the water.

The **Harvest Mouse** has been driven out of cornfields by farm machinery. Nowadays it often sleeps in reed beds. This mouse is an expert climber and can hang by its tail. It comes out in the daytime.

This bat often flies over water in the daytime, hunting for insects. It can swim well too.

Daubenton's Bat

The **Brown Rat** prefers rivers and canals. Look for it at any time of day. It eats almost anything.

The **Water Shrew** sometimes leaps out of the water to catch insects. It also eats fish and frogs. You may see it walking on the bottom of streams, looking for food.

Look for plant stems which have been bitten off. These could be clues to the feeding spot of a **Water Vole**.

Holes in the bank, either above or below water, could be the entrance to a **Shrew's** or **Vole's** burrow.

Rare water mammals

Muskrat

Beaver

European Mink

The Muskrat is a large vole that lives in parts of Europe, but not in Britain. It swims fast and keeps near the surface of shallow, overgrown water.

A few Beavers survive in Europe, mostly in remote northern areas. They build their homes, called lodges, with branches or logs that they cut from trees.

Some Mink are wild. Others have escaped from fur farms. You might see one in a reed bed or by a river. They hunt and swim at night. They are very fierce.

Otter

Waterproof fur

Spraints

When it dives for fish, it shuts its ears and nostrils.

Webbed toes for swimming.

Its thick tail acts as a rudder.

The Otter is a shy, nocturnal animal. It lives in lonely places, and is well suited to life in the water. It eats fish, frogs and shellfish. Otter cubs are born in a tunnel,

called a holt, in a bank or among tree roots. They are very playful and make slides down the river bank in the mud or snow. You might see one of these

slides, or find Otter droppings, called spraints, on a rock or clump of grass. Otters often leave behind remains of fish they have eaten.

Tracks

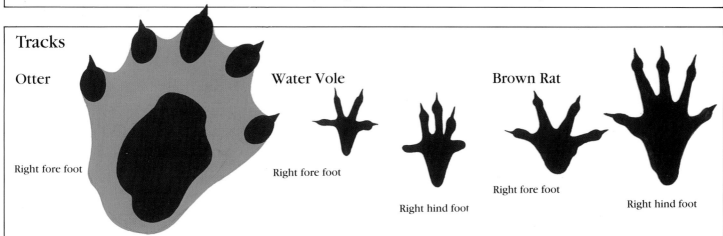

Otter

Right fore foot

Water Vole

Right fore foot

Right hind foot

Brown Rat

Right fore foot

Right hind foot

Look for animal tracks in firm mud or snow. The best time to look is in the morning, before the fresh tracks have been spoiled.

To help you identify them later, measure and draw the tracks, and the pattern, or trail, the tracks make together. Remember that you will not find a

complete track showing all of the animal's foot, very often. An Otter track, for instance, may not show the web, claw marks or even the fifth toe.

Fish

Some types of freshwater fish prefer still water and other types prefer moving water. Make a check-list to help you to identify the different types. What colour and shape are they? Do they have whiskers, or barbels, near the mouth? Do they live at the surface or on the bottom? How fast do they swim?

Most freshwater fish lay their eggs, called spawning, in shallow water. Look for eggs among water plants, and on the water's bottom. Young fish are called fry.

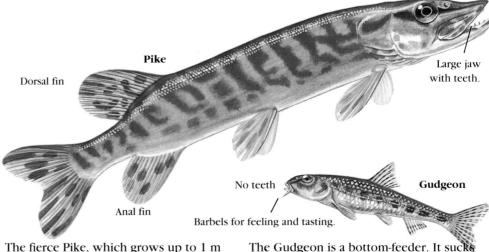

Pike

Dorsal fin

Large jaw with teeth.

Anal fin

No teeth

Barbels for feeling and tasting.

Gudgeon

The fierce Pike, which grows up to 1 m long, hunts frogs, young birds, fish, and even other Pike. It lurks in reeds, waiting for its prey, and then attacks with its sharp teeth.

The Gudgeon is a bottom-feeder. It sucks insect larvae, worms and shellfish into its mouth. There are no teeth in the mouth, but it has teeth in its throat which break up the food it swallows.

In a pond

Most pond fish are rounder and fatter than the slim, streamlined fish in moving water. They swim more slowly too.

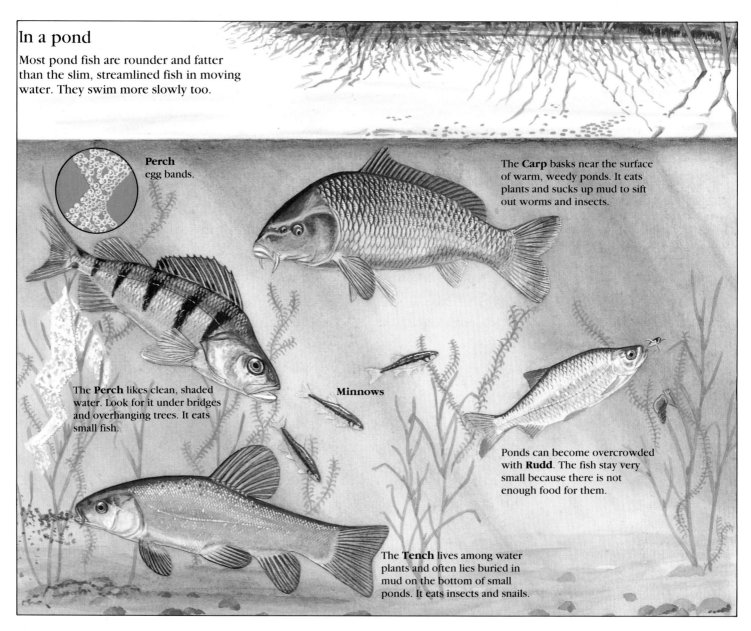

Perch egg bands.

The Carp basks near the surface of warm, weedy ponds. It eats plants and sucks up mud to sift out worms and insects.

The **Perch** likes clean, shaded water. Look for it under bridges and overhanging trees. It eats small fish.

Minnows

Ponds can become overcrowded with **Rudd**. The fish stay very small because there is not enough food for them.

The **Tench** lives among water plants and often lies buried in mud on the bottom of small ponds. It eats insects and snails.

Building a nest

Three-spined Stickleback

Male

The male has a red throat and belly in the breeding season.

Female

Male

Male

Look for the Three-spined Stickleback in ponds and ditches. In May, a male builds a nest where the female will lay her eggs. He glues bits of plants together with sticky threads from his body. The male "dances" to attract a female to the nest. When the female has laid her eggs, she leaves the nest. The male then fans the eggs with his fins to keep fresh water flowing over them. When the eggs hatch, the male guards the fry and chases away enemies. When one of the baby fish strays away from the nest, he follows it. Then, catching the fry in his mouth, he brings it back to the nest.

In a stream

The **Dace** is often found in large schools near the surface of the water.

The **Grayling** has a large dorsal fin. It eats insect larvae. It cannot live in polluted water.

The small **Minnow** often moves about in groups, called schools. It is eaten by other fish and by water birds.

Trout live in fast-flowing streams. Their dark spots act as a camouflage on the stony bottom.

The **Bullhead** hides under stones in the day. It comes out at night to feed on insect larvae and small shellfish.

Eels

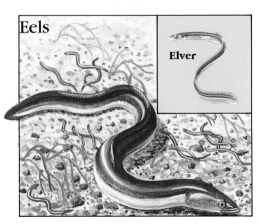

Elver

Eels live in fresh water until they are about ten years old. Then they move down the river into the sea, to breed and die. The young eels, called elvers, travel back to fresh water.

Salmon

Salmon spend some of their lives in the sea, but return to the rivers to breed. Often they go back to the river where they were born. The female lays up to 15,000 eggs on the river bottom.

Remember!

If you want to see fish, approach the water slowly and quietly. Keep your shadow off the water. Try feeding fish with bread or maggots.

Frogs, toads and newts

Frogs, toads and newts are born in water, but spend most of their adult life on land. These types of animals are called amphibians.

Young amphibians, called tadpoles, develop from eggs, called spawn. These are laid in the water. They breathe by taking in oxygen from the water through their gills. As they grow, their gills and tails disappear and lungs and legs develop. Newt tadpoles keep their tails. Eventually, they leave the water, but return in the spring to breed.

Frogs

Common Frog

Smooth moist skin.

Long tongue joined to the front of the mouth.

Dark patches around its ears and on its back legs.

Webbed toes for swimming.

Long back legs for jumping.

The Common Frog lives in damp grass and undergrowth. Its basic skin colour can change to match its surroundings. This helps it to hide from snakes, hedgehogs, rats and other enemies. In winter, the frog hibernates in the mud bottom of a ditch or pond. It shoots out its long tongue to catch flies.

How frogs breed

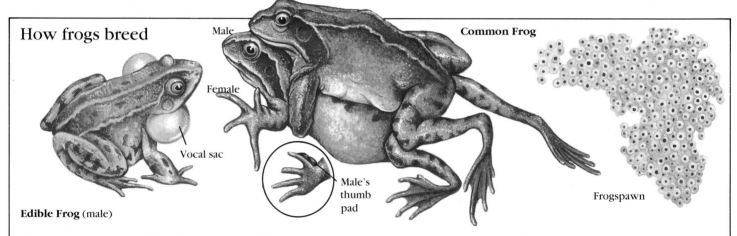

Male

Female

Vocal sac

Male's thumb pad

Edible Frog (male)

Common Frog

Frogspawn

Frogs breed in ponds. Male frogs croak to attract females. The male Edible Frog makes his croak sound louder by blowing up his vocal sacs.

When mating, the male frog holds on to the female with his spiky thumb pads. The female lays a clump of frogspawn in the water.

A clump of frogspawn contains up to 4,000 eggs. The jelly absorbs water and swells up and floats to the surface, where the sun warms the eggs.

How frogspawn develops

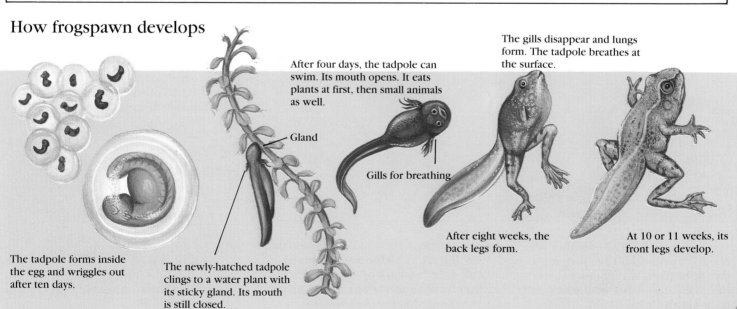

After four days, the tadpole can swim. Its mouth opens. It eats plants at first, then small animals as well.

Gland

Gills for breathing

The gills disappear and lungs form. The tadpole breathes at the surface.

The tadpole forms inside the egg and wriggles out after ten days.

The newly-hatched tadpole clings to a water plant with its sticky gland. Its mouth is still closed.

After eight weeks, the back legs form.

At 10 or 11 weeks, its front legs develop.

Toads

Common Toad

Toads have blunter faces and fatter bodies than frogs.

Poison on the skin helps to ward off enemies.

Dry, warty skin.

Old skin being eaten.

Short back legs for crawling.

During the day, the Common Toad hides in holes in the ground, but at night hunts for food. It grows a new skin several times in the summer. It scrapes off the old one and eats it. In winter, the toad hibernates in an old animal burrow.

Danger

Toad

Grass Snake

If a toad is threatened by a Grass Snake, it may blow itself up so that the snake cannot swallow it.

Toadspawn

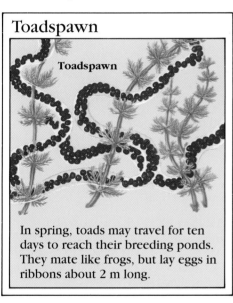

Toadspawn

In spring, toads may travel for ten days to reach their breeding ponds. They mate like frogs, but lay eggs in ribbons about 2 m long.

At 12 or 13 weeks, the tail disappears and the tiny frog, 1 cm long, is ready to leave the water. It will be fully grown in three years. Few tadpoles survive to this stage. Most are eaten by other pond creatures.

Newts

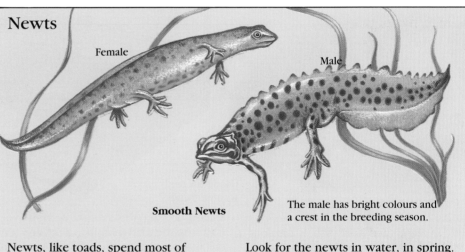

Female

Male

Smooth Newts

The male has bright colours and a crest in the breeding season.

Newts, like toads, spend most of their life on land, hiding by day and feeding at night. They look rather like lizards, but are not scaly.

Look for the newts in water, in spring. You might see the male Smooth Newt performing his courtship dance. He arches his back and flicks his tail.

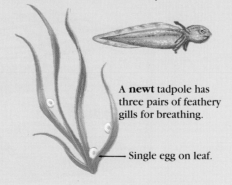

Its front legs grow first. The tadpole eats water fleas and tiny worms.

A **newt** tadpole has three pairs of feathery gills for breathing.

Single egg on leaf.

The gills disappear and its lungs and back legs develop.

Newts lay their eggs singly, on water plants. The leaves are often bent over to protect the eggs. The tadpoles hatch after about two weeks. The young newts, called efts, leave the water in August. Some stay in the water until the next year.

Keeping amphibians

Frogspawn

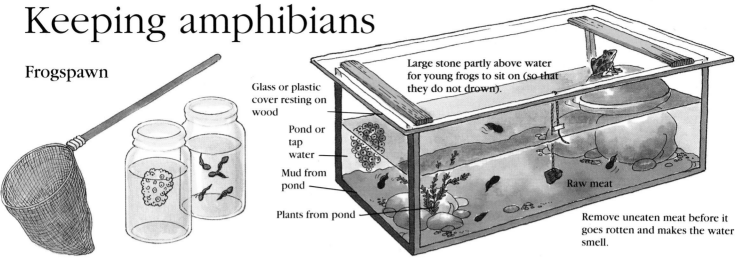

Large stone partly above water for young frogs to sit on (so that they do not drown).

Glass or plastic cover resting on wood

Pond or tap water

Mud from pond

Plants from pond

Raw meat

Remove uneaten meat before it goes rotten and makes the water smell.

Look in ponds in March and April. Use a net to collect frogspawn. Put a little in a jar of water and return the rest to the pond. If the eggs have already hatched, collect a few tadpoles to study instead.

Put the aquarium in a light place, but out of direct sunlight. Change the water as soon as it smells bad. When the frogs have grown, return them to the edge of the pond where you found the spawn.

Newly-hatched tadpoles will eat plants in the aquarium. After about a week, they will need raw meat too. Hang small pieces in the water, tied with thread, and replace them every two days.

Toads

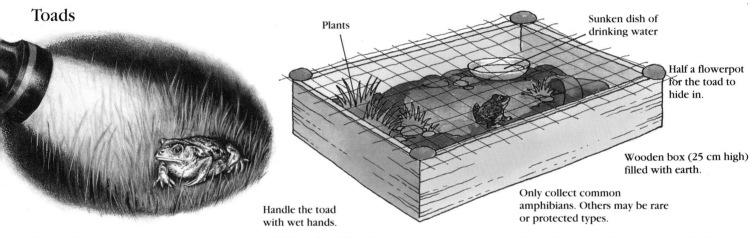

Plants

Sunken dish of drinking water

Half a flowerpot for the toad to hide in.

Wooden box (25 cm high) filled with earth.

Only collect common amphibians. Others may be rare or protected types.

Handle the toad with wet hands.

During the breeding season, visit ponds at night in March and April. When a male toad croaks, shine a torch at him, and he will freeze. Take him home in a wet plastic box with air holes.

Make a box like this and put netting over it to stop the toad jumping out. Keep it in the shade, either in the garden or indoors. Return it to the pond's edge, in the autumn, so it can hibernate.

Feed the toad twice a week with live earthworms, slugs and insects. Offer it small pieces of meat held in tweezers and move it about to make it look alive. Keep the dish filled with fresh water.

Newts

Stick for fishing rod

Cotton line

Matchstick float

Worm

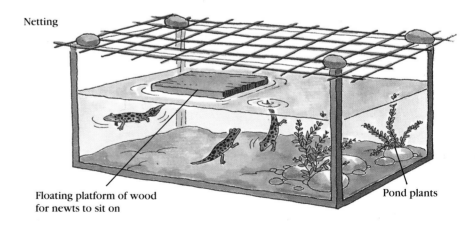

Netting

Floating platform of wood for newts to sit on

Pond plants

In early spring, fish for newts or catch them in a net. When the newt bites the worm bait, pull the line in. Take it home in a jar with some pond water. Do not collect rare types of newt.

Keep newts in an aquarium in a light place, but not in direct sunlight. In August, take them back to the edge of the same pond, so that they can find a place to hibernate during the cold months.

Feed young newts and tadpoles on Water Fleas from the pond. Feed adult newts on earthworms and small bits of raw meat dropped into the water. Keep a diary as the young develop and grow.

Other water animals

Worms and leeches

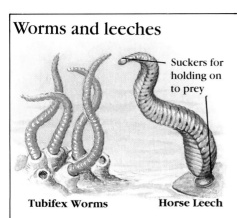

Suckers for holding on to prey

Tubifex Worms   **Horse Leech**

There are many kinds of worms and leeches in fresh water. The Tubifex Worm lives head down in a tube of mud. Leeches swim about hunting for fish, frogs, insect larvae and snails.

Hydras

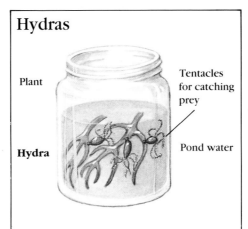

Plant

Hydra

Tentacles for catching prey

Pond water

These tiny plant-like animals contract into blobs when disturbed. Leave some water plants in water for an hour to see if there are any Hydras attached to them.

Spiders and mites

Water Spider   Bubble of air   **Water Mites**

The Water Spider is the only spider to live under water. It spins a web between plants, then fills it with air collected on its body from the surface. The spider can stay in this "diving bell" for a long time, without surfacing for air. Look for the tiny Water Mites which are related to the spider family.

Animals with shells

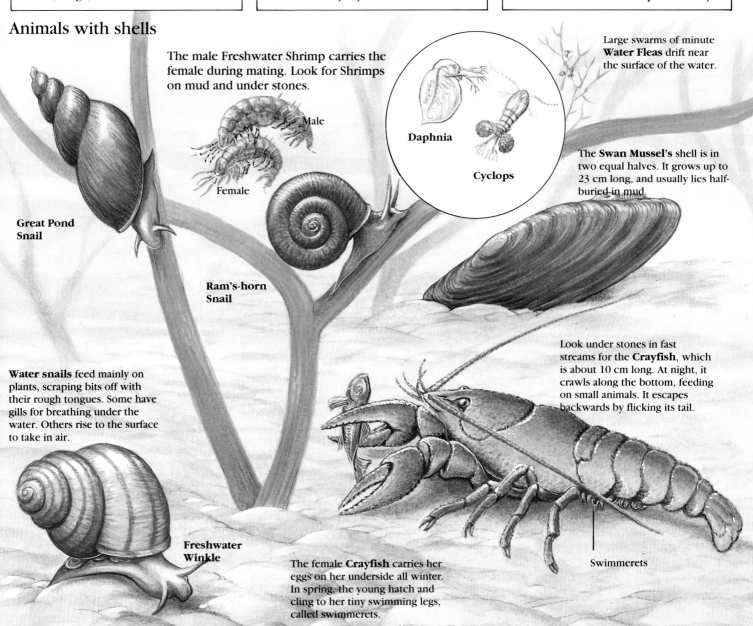

The male Freshwater Shrimp carries the female during mating. Look for Shrimps on mud and under stones.

Male

Female

Large swarms of minute **Water Fleas** drift near the surface of the water.

Daphnia

Cyclops

The **Swan Mussel's** shell is in two equal halves. It grows up to 23 cm long, and usually lies half-buried in mud.

Great Pond Snail

Ram's-horn Snail

Water snails feed mainly on plants, scraping bits off with their rough tongues. Some have gills for breathing under the water. Others rise to the surface to take in air.

Look under stones in fast streams for the **Crayfish**, which is about 10 cm long. At night, it crawls along the bottom, feeding on small animals. It escapes backwards by flicking its tail.

Freshwater Winkle

The female **Crayfish** carries her eggs on her underside all winter. In spring, the young hatch and cling to her tiny swimming legs, called swimmerets.

Swimmerets

More freshwater life you can spot

Fish

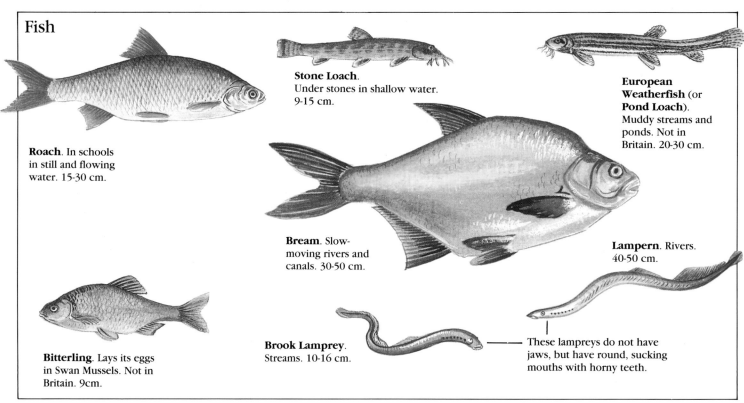

Stone Loach. Under stones in shallow water. 9-15 cm.

European Weatherfish (or **Pond Loach**). Muddy streams and ponds. Not in Britain. 20-30 cm.

Roach. In schools in still and flowing water. 15-30 cm.

Bream. Slow-moving rivers and canals. 30-50 cm.

Lampern. Rivers. 40-50 cm.

Bitterling. Lays its eggs in Swan Mussels. Not in Britain. 9cm.

Brook Lamprey. Streams. 10-16 cm.

These lampreys do not have jaws, but have round, sucking mouths with horny teeth.

Plants

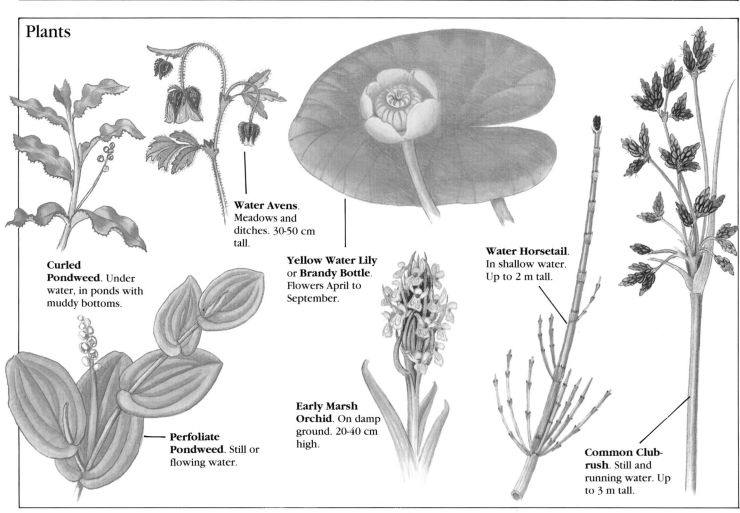

Water Avens. Meadows and ditches. 30-50 cm tall.

Curled Pondweed. Under water, in ponds with muddy bottoms.

Yellow Water Lily or **Brandy Bottle**. Flowers April to September.

Water Horsetail. In shallow water. Up to 2 m tall.

Perfoliate Pondweed. Still or flowing water.

Early Marsh Orchid. On damp ground. 20-40 cm high.

Common Club-rush. Still and running water. Up to 3 m tall.

If you cannot see the fish or plant you want to identify on this page, turn to the pages earlier in the book that may deal with it.

Toads

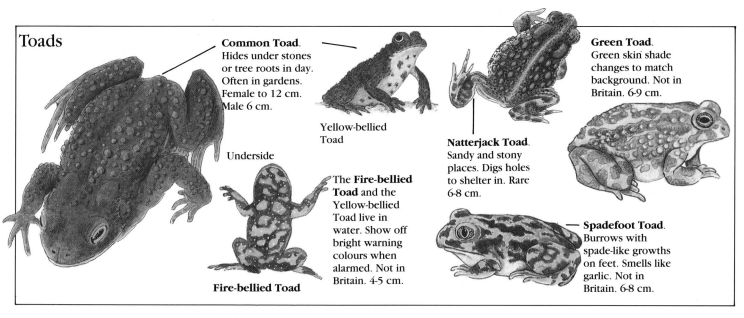

Common Toad. Hides under stones or tree roots in day. Often in gardens. Female to 12 cm. Male 6 cm.

Yellow-bellied Toad

Underside

The **Fire-bellied Toad** and the Yellow-bellied Toad live in water. Show off bright warning colours when alarmed. Not in Britain. 4-5 cm.

Fire-bellied Toad

Natterjack Toad. Sandy and stony places. Digs holes to shelter in. Rare 6-8 cm.

Green Toad. Green skin shade changes to match background. Not in Britain. 6-9 cm.

Spadefoot Toad. Burrows with spade-like growths on feet. Smells like garlic. Not in Britain. 6-8 cm.

Frogs

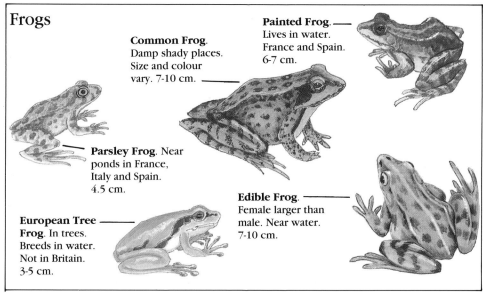

Common Frog. Damp shady places. Size and colour vary. 7-10 cm.

Painted Frog. Lives in water. France and Spain. 6-7 cm.

Parsley Frog. Near ponds in France, Italy and Spain. 4.5 cm.

European Tree Frog. In trees. Breeds in water. Not in Britain. 3-5 cm.

Edible Frog. Female larger than male. Near water. 7-10 cm.

Tortoise

European Pond Tortoise. Muddy ponds and marshes. Central and southern Europe. Up to 36 cm.

Newts

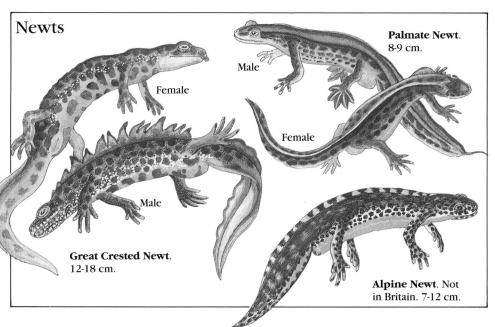

Female

Male

Palmate Newt. 8-9 cm.

Female

Great Crested Newt. 12-18 cm.

Male

Alpine Newt. Not in Britain. 7-12 cm.

Snakes

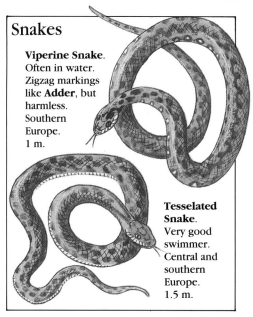

Viperine Snake. Often in water. Zigzag markings like **Adder**, but harmless. Southern Europe. 1 m.

Tesselated Snake. Very good swimmer. Central and southern Europe. 1.5 m.

All these frogs, toads and newts return to water to breed.

Water insects and their young

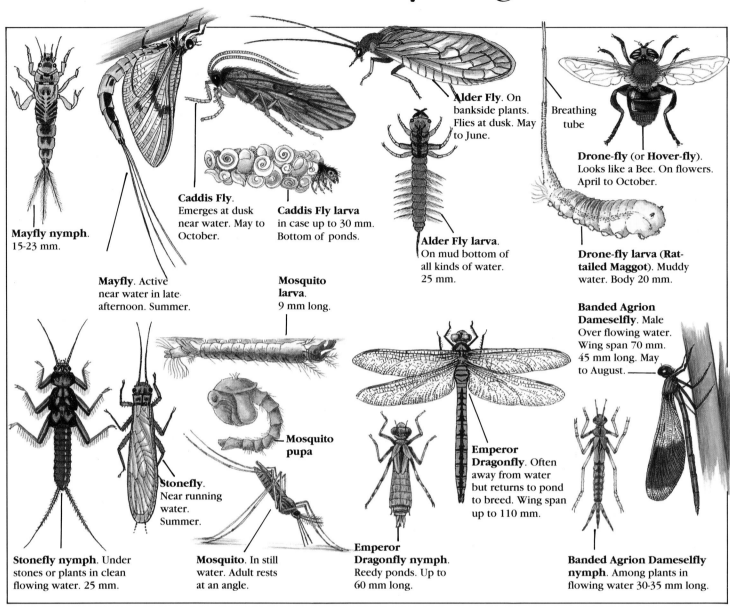

Mayfly nymph. 15-23 mm.

Mayfly. Active near water in late afternoon. Summer.

Caddis Fly. Emerges at dusk near water. May to October.

Caddis Fly larva in case up to 30 mm. Bottom of ponds.

Mosquito larva. 9 mm long.

Alder Fly. On bankside plants. Flies at dusk. May to June.

Alder Fly larva. On mud bottom of all kinds of water. 25 mm.

Breathing tube

Drone-fly (or Hover-fly). Looks like a Bee. On flowers. April to October.

Drone-fly larva (Rat-tailed Maggot). Muddy water. Body 20 mm.

Banded Agrion Dameselfly. Male Over flowing water. Wing span 70 mm. 45 mm long. May to August.

Mosquito pupa

Stonefly. Near running water. Summer.

Emperor Dragonfly. Often away from water but returns to pond to breed. Wing span up to 110 mm.

Stonefly nymph. Under stones or plants in clean flowing water. 25 mm.

Mosquito. In still water. Adult rests at an angle.

Emperor Dragonfly nymph. Reedy ponds. Up to 60 mm long.

Banded Agrion Dameselfly nymph. Among plants in flowing water 30-35 mm long.

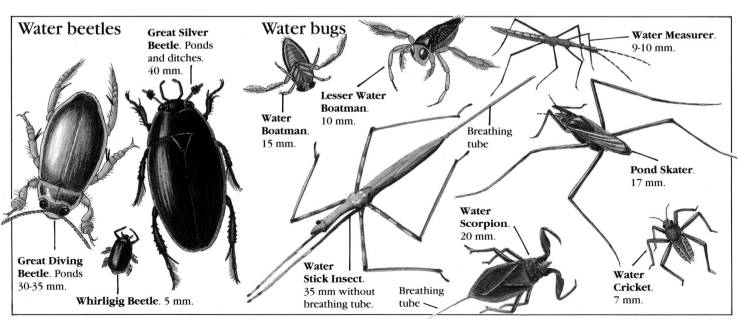

Water beetles

Great Silver Beetle. Ponds and ditches. 40 mm.

Water bugs

Water Measurer. 9-10 mm.

Lesser Water Boatman. 10 mm.

Water Boatman. 15 mm.

Breathing tube

Pond Skater. 17 mm.

Great Diving Beetle. Ponds 30-35 mm.

Whirligig Beetle. 5 mm.

Water Stick Insect. 35 mm without breathing tube.

Breathing tube

Water Scorpion. 20 mm.

Water Cricket. 7 mm.

If you cannot see the insect you want to identify here, turn to the pages earlier in the book on insects. You may be able to see a picture of it there.

Birds

Measurements are from beak to tip of tail.

Grey Heron. Nests in trees. Feeds in shallow water and marshes. 90 cm.

Osprey. Dives to catch fish in claws. Rare. A few breed in Scotland. 51-58 cm.

Great Crested Grebe. In lakes and reservoirs. Winters also on coast. 48 cm.

Winter

Summer

Mallard. Most common duck. Often in parks. 58 cm.

Female

Male

Chick

Teal. Europe's smallest duck. 35 cm.

Female

Male

Chick

Coot. Lives in flocks outside breeding season. Notice white mark on head. 38 cm.

Chick

Moorhen. Common in parks. Notice white flash under tail. 33 cm.

Snipe. Hides among plants near water, where it feeds. Long bill for probing in mud. 27 cm.

Water Rail. Hides in reed beds. 28 cm.

Summer

Winter

Black-headed Gull. Loses dark cap in winter. 35-38 cm.

Spotted Crake. White spotted body. Feeds at water edge at dusk. Very secretive. 23 cm.

Swallow. Summer visitor. Catches insects on the wing. 19 cm.

Yellow Wagtail. Lives in Britain. Blue-headed Wagtail in Central Europe. Other varieties in Europe (see below). 16.5 cm.

Yellow Wagtail

Pied wagtail

Female

Blue headed wagtail

White Wagtail

Male

Scandinavia

Italy

Spain and France

Grey Wagtail. Lives near fast-flowing streams. 18 cm.

White Wagtail. Lives in Europe. Pied Wagtail in Britain. 18 cm.

Reed Bunting. By rivers and in marshy places. 15 cm.

If you cannot see the bird you want to identify here, turn to the pages earlier in the book on birds, and you may be able to see a picture of it there.

Index

Books to read

Collins Field Guide to Freshwater Life.
  Richard Fitter and Richard Manuel
  (Collins)
The Pond. Gerald Thompson, Jennifer
  Coldrey and George Bernard (Collins)
Field Guide to the Water Life of Britain.
  (Reader's Digest Nature Lover's
  Library)
Collins Green Guides - books include
  Fish, Insects, Birds, Wild Flowers, and
  Trees. (Collins)
Britain's Wildlife, Plants and Flowers - A
  Complete Spotter's Guide. (Reader's
  Digest)
Observer's Birds. Hume (Penguin)

Clubs and national organizations

The Council for Environmental Conservation (80 York Way, London, N1 9AG) will supply the addresses of your local **Natural History Societies**. Send an s.a.e. for the list.
The Royal Society for the Protection of Nature (Vigilant House, 120 Wilton Road, London SW1V 1J2) will give you the address of your local **County Naturalist Trust**, which may have a junior branch. Many of the Trusts have meetings and lectures, and offer opportunities for work on nature reserves.
The Young Ornithologists' Club (RSPB,

The Lodge, Sandy, Bedfordshire SG19 2DL) is a national club for young birdwatchers.
Freshwater Biological Association, The Ferry House, Far Sawrey, Ambleside, Cumbria, LA22 0LP
The Botanical Society of the British Isles, c/o Natural History Museum, Cromwell Road, London, SW7 5BD
English Nature, Northminster House, Peterborough OE1 1UA
The Countryside Commission, John Dower House, Crescent Place, Cheltenham, Gloucestershire GL50 3RA